Unfinished Painting is the 1988 Lamont Poetry Selection of the Academy of American Poets.

From 1954 through 1974 the Lamont Poetry Selection supported the publication and distribution of twenty first books of poems. Since 1975 this distinguished award has been given for an American poet's second book.

Judges for 1988: *Alfred Corn, Sandra McPherson,* and *Mary Oliver.*

BOOKS BY MARY JO SALTER

Unfinished Painting   1989

Henry Purcell in Japan   1985

UNFINISHED PAINTING

Unfinished Painting

P O E M S   B Y

Mary Jo Salter

ALFRED A. KNOPF   NEW YORK   1989

THIS IS A BORZOI BOOK
PUBLISHED BY ALFRED A. KNOPF, INC.

ACKNOWLEDGMENTS Thanks to the editors of the following magazines, where these poems (sometimes in different form) appeared:

The Atlantic Monthly   The Upper Story

Crosscurrents   I Lose You for an Instant

Grand Street   Late Spring, Puzzle Piece, Elegies for Etsuko (*as* Etsuko: An Elegy)

The New Criterion   Unfinished Painting

The New Republic   Dead Letters

The New Yorker   Spring Thaw in South Hadley, Summer 1983, A Case of Netsuke

Oxford Poetry   The Rebirth of Venus

Southwest Review   Emily Wants to Play, Aubade for Brad

Yale Review   The Annunciation, The Moon and Big Ben

I am grateful to the National Endowment for the Arts, for a poetry fellowship, and to the MacDowell Colony, for the time and place to work on some of these poems. Of a number of people who offered encouragement and advice, I am particularly thankful to two editors, Ann Close and Alice Quinn, and two poets, Amy Clampitt and Brad Leithauser.

Library of Congress Cataloging-in-Publication Data

Salter, Mary Jo.
    Unfinished painting: poems/by Mary Jo Salter.
        p.   cm.
    ISBN 0-394-57417-6 (clothbound)
         0-679-72298-x (paperback)
        I. Title.
PS3569.A46224U64   1989   88-45802
811'.54—dc19   CIP

Manufactured in the United States of America
First Edition

To the memory of my mother,
LORMINA PARADISE SALTER
1924–1983

CONTENTS

I

UNFINISHED PAINTING

THE REBIRTH OF VENUS

He's knelt to fish her face up from the sidewalk
all morning, and at last some shoppers gather
to see it drawn—wide-eyed, and dry as chalk—
whole from the sea of dreams. It's she. None other

than the other one who's copied in the book
he copies from, that woman men divined
ages before a painter let them look
into the eyes their eyes had had in mind.

Love's called him too, today, though she has taught
him in her beauty to love best
the one who first had formed her from a thought.
One square of pavement, like a headstone (lest

anyone mistake where credit lies),
reads BOTTICELLI, but the long-closed dates
suggest, instead, a view of centuries
coming unbracketed, as if the gates

might swing wide to admit, here, in the sun,
one humble man into the pantheon
older and more exalted than her own.
    Slow gods of Art, late into afternoon

let there be light: a few of us drop the wish
into his glinting coinbox like a well,
remembering the forecast. Yet he won't rush
her finish, though it means she'll have no shell

to harbor in; it's clear enough the rain
will swamp her like a tide, and lion-hearted
he'll set off, black umbrella sprung again,
envisioning faces where the streets have parted.

SPRING THAW IN SOUTH HADLEY

Old snows locked under glass
by last night's ice storm left
curatorial Winter, in
whose hands alone we'd hope
to find the keys,
jangling them in the trees—

not merely in these pine
needles by the fistful
gloved in crystal, but,
from their boughs, the self-
invented digits of
icicles addressed

(in a manner reminiscent
of the insubstantial
finger of a sundial)
less to a point in space
than effectively to Time,
the frozen moment.

By noon, the ice as thin
as an eggshell veined to show
life seeping yellow,
one's boots sink in
with a snap; the sap
underrunning everything

may be nothing but water, yet
there's a sacramental
joy in how, converting
to its liquid state,
it's anything but gentle.
A crash from Abbey Chapel—

who cut the string
that sent the white sheets falling?
Nothing but the long
scissors of the sun
unwraps such thunder. Even
a modest A-frame

in a muffled instant sheds
its wrinkling roofs of snow:
black butterfly below.
As if to make
one more clean break above,
the sky—seconds ago

one continent of cloud—
follows the drift of Spring,
splits and refits like Ming
porcelain. The plate
tectonics alternate:
white and blue, blue and white.

READING ROOM

Williston Memorial Library,
Mount Holyoke College

The chapter ends. And when I look up
from a sunken pose in an easy chair
(half, or more than half, asleep?)
the height and heft of the room come back;
darkly, the pitched ceiling falls
forward like a book.
Even those mock-Tudor stripes
have come to seem like unread lines.
Oh, what I haven't read!

—and how the room, importunate
as a church, leans as if reading *me*:
the three high windows in the shape
of a bishop's cap, and twenty girls
jutting from the walls like gargoyles
or (more kindly) guardian angels
that peer over the shoulder, straight
into the heart. Wooden girls who exist
only above the waist—

whose wings fuse thickly into poles
behind them—they hold against their breasts,
alternately, books or scrolls
turned outward, as if they mean to ask:
Have you done your Rhetoric today?
Your passage of Scripture? Your Natural
Philosophy? In their arch, archaic
silence, one can't help but hear a
mandate from another era,

and all too easy to discount
for sounding quaint. Poor
Emily Dickinson, when she was here,
had to report on the progress of
her soul toward Christ. (She said: *No hope.*)
Just as well no one demands
to know *that* any more . . . Yet
one attends, as to a lecture,
to this stern-faced architecture—

Duty is Truth, Truth Duty—as one
doesn't to the whitewashed, low
ceilings of our own. Despite
the air these angels have of being
knowing (which mainly comes by virtue
of there being less to know back then),
there's modesty in how they flank
the room like twenty figureheads;
they won't, or can't, reveal who leads

the ship you need to board. Beneath
lamps dangled from the angels' hands—
stars to steer us who knows where—
thousands of periodicals
unfurl their thin, long-winded sails;
back there, in the unlovely stacks,
the books sleep cramped as sailors.
So little time to learn what's worth
our time! No one to climb that stair

and stop there, on the balcony
walled like a pulpit or a king's
outlook in a fairy tale,
to set three tasks, to pledge rewards.
Even the angels, after all,
whose burning lamps invoke a quest
further into the future, drive
us back to assimilate the past
before we lose the words.

No, nobody in the pulpit
but for the built-in, oaken face
of a timepiece that—I check my watch—
still works. As roundly useful as
the four-armed ceiling fans that keep
even the air in circulation,
it plays by turns with hope and doubt;
hard not to read here, in the clock's
crossed hands, the paradox

of Time that is forever running out.

THE UPPER STORY

As Emily Dickinson
would not come down, I'm
sorry, but I've felt the need to climb
the worn steps to her room,
winding up the stair
as if into her inner ear.

Art, as she once said,
is *a House that tries to be haunted,*
and as I stand
on the landing where she curled in shadow
to follow the piano
and soprano voice of Mabel Todd

(her editor years later—
who now graciously accepted
a poem and glass of sherry in place
of having seen her face),
this would become that House.
No trespass can erase

what she once made of it—
that gate she opened, resolute
to escape, and just as quickly shut:
*I think I was held in check by some
invisible agent . . . And when she wrote
Again—his voice is at the door—*

here is the door she meant.
Her room, probably Spartan
even when lived in, now holds but few
fabled artifacts: a snow-white
coverlet; a "sleigh bed," narrow
like a wooden shoe; a snipped

lily of a dress, limp in the closet;
a wilted hatbox; a woven basket
she'd lower, something like Rapunzel,
full of gingerbread.
Or so our guide has said. Yet
devoted to the genuine

as she was—first jasmine of the season,
hummingbird and snake—
I doubt she would have taken umbrage
when learned men in Cambridge
spirited off her writing table
to higher education. A double

(its surface little more
than two feet square, and where
poems commensurately small
were scrawled on backs of envelopes)
sits convincingly beneath the tall
window onto Main Street.

To shut our eyes is Travel,
and that table may as well
be anywhere as here.
She'd have held close whatever house
she was born in, as a squirrel
palms its acorn; but with a need

not wholly fed by fear.
At twenty-four, moving back
to her birthplace, she'd lived the thought
transposed: To travel, shut the eyes.
I supposed we were going to make a "transit,"
as heavenly bodies did . . .

She was truly half-
astonished at those carriages
and cartons—almost as if
she'd lived only in that other life,
unseen, in her upper story.
Touch Shakespeare for me,

she wrote to Mabel in Europe,
thinking her close enough.
Why had anyone expressed the hope
to see Emily, who'd compare in letters
her unmet friends to Peter's
Christ: "whom having not seen, ye love"?

Finding nothing and no time
impalpable, she'd call
attention to the Biblical
"house not made with hands" for all
who'd listen. Wasn't that her home
as much as this was? Fame,

a lower form of Immortality,
in the intervening century
has unpacked her cradle to restore
its place, steps from her deathbed.
There is no first, or last, in Forever . . .
To the West, across the field

from another window, lives the family
at The Evergreens, whom Emily
saw little more than I can: Austin
and dark sister-in-law Sue.
I would have come out of Eden
to open the Door for you . . .

but she hadn't had to.
Drumming down the stair,
my ears fill with the spirals of a fly
a poem let in and won't be shown the way:
as if that buzzing, when she died,
were here still amplified.

THE ANNUNCIATION

Unparalleled on Earth, their faces look
alike—like open pages from the Book
wherein their story's told as was foretold,
since prophecies are made to be recalled;
like Gabriel's wings, one iridescent, one
behind illumined purely by assumption.
He, gazing in her eyes, taught all that he

might teach her of divine tautology
the moment when his profile met the plane
her profile had established first as human.
They do it all with mirrors: odd to conceive
her image in our other mother, Eve,
and yet what's odd must, doubled, come out even—
like unlikely Eden, verified by Heaven.

"LATE SPRING"

(Li Shih-Cho, ca. 1690–1770)

The way a breeze blows
  open a pleated skirt, the fan
    expands. And splay in that wide-angled lens,
  a scene unfolds of smaller fans:
of cowlicked shoots of rice

rising up from honey-
  combed terraces; of burled willows in
    the truncated forefront, whose furthest branches turn
  yet more delicate in arcs
filigreed by green.

Unlike those hanging scrolls
  of tall, unrolling waterfalls
    and a fisherman who, by a tributary, nods
  too far from the cataracts to hear,
almost out of the picture,

or the narratives of lives
  on the horizontal, a pilgrimage
    of tales on a reel that splices years to years—
  the boy astride his goat, the ancient
praying at the shrine

in one continuous line—
  this fan cuts a pie-shaped slice of life
    as seen not by God, nor the compound eye of the housefly;
  it's no more, or less, than a person can
compass at a glance.

Yet were we to dig
   from China down to Leeuwenhoek,
     at work, a handful of springs before, on fields
   of vision yet unharvested,
we'd find the subdivided source

of metaphors (the lace
   of skin, for instance—rhombuses
     any whichway stitched to triangles
   in a perfectly systemic mesh
of irregularity,

so that even the finest
   designs in us sew up the case
     against the perfectibility of man)
   that surface now to consciousness.
As here: a myriad

of paddied cells elongate
   in climbing to the horizon, and
     finally, seen sideways, flatten dry.
   Up close, too decorous to tread
on puddled nuclei

of rice, a gentleman little
   larger than a ladybug
     traces a lane of ink-line; in the bifocal
   Oriental tradition of
looked-in-on solitude—

the fisherman, the sage
   high in his hermitage, or even
      the swan that, as the sun does, trails ellipses
   in her wake, but in a pond
all hers, unplaneted—

his being alone is so
   delicious you want to join him; no,
      to be him; or, best, to be him and yet
   stand back, here and now, relishing
him in that long-drawn Spring.

It's clear he doesn't see,
   as we have learned to, ply on ply,
      the paisley of amoebas hidden in
   the fabric of Creation's fan
that folds up into One;

indeed, although he'd seem
   more likely than we to note the yellow
      oriole perched, three paintdrops, in that willow,
   his face, as rendered, is so
small he has no eyes at all.

A CASE OF NETSUKE

Wise, size of a peachpit, nut-
brown, wizened, intricate,
   the Badger Dressed in Lotus Leaf
stands tall in his sheet: as grand
or grander than Rodin's Balzac, and

even smacks of evil, as
he has the full, unruffled gaze
   of the Wolf under Grandmother's nightgown.
The better to draw you close, my dear,
to a museum-case of obscure

Japanese bibelots. Each
a tangible anecdote, they reach
   first to us from English tags:
Starving Dog, Herdboy with Flute,
Dutchman with Moneybag, or Stoat

on Pumpkin, Bean Pods, Pile of Fish . . .
As if that wordless, brimming wish
   to get everything said before
we're dead might be fulfilled at last,
they speak to us of a lost

life we may have lived once, though
it's daunting we should think so—
   for what could we have had in common
with Seated Demon or Drunken Sprite?
And by what twist does Thwarted Rat-

Catcher call up the aim of Art?
Yet that look of his, of being thwarted,
    as he crouches over the empty cage
and, too late, lifts his club to thwack
the rat scaling his own back,

is intimately familiar—like
the downturned, howling mask of tragic
    theater. If somehow the play
of his features also shows he's half-
laughing, it may be at himself:

grinning, with a shrunken skull's
grim triumph, or like a set of false
    teeth that's doubled over in
age-yellowed ivory,
he's detached from his unsavory

and blunt stabs at success. The gift,
he chides himself, is to be swift
    and tireless; to hit on a connection—
not just pummel the rat but tell
the whole tale in a nutshell.

UNFINISHED PAINTING

Dark son, whose face once shone like this,
oiled from well within the skin
of canvas, and whose liquid eyes
were brown as rootbeer underneath
    a crewcut's crown, just washed,

his body's gone unfinished now
more than thirty years—blank tent
of bathrobe like a choirboy's surplice
over the cassock's stroke of color,
    a red pajama collar.

Drawn as if it might reveal
the dotted hills of Rome, a drape
behind him opens on a wall
she'd painted with a roller once.
    Everything made at home—

she made the drapes, she made the boy,
and then, pure joy, remade him in
a pose to bear his mother's hope:
the deep, three-quarter gaze; the tome
    he fingers like a pope.

Is this the History of Art
he marks her place in, or—wait—
that illustrated Brothers Grimm
she'd inscribed for him, his name enclosed
    within it like a heart?

Hard to sort out . . . She rarely put
the final touch on anything
when he was young. It seems that bringing
the real boy up had taken time
    away from painting him

(no crime); she'd also failed to think
of him—back then her only child—
as truly done, and one child only,
but marvelled as he altered like
    the light she painted by.

. . . Like, too, the image he's retained
of the sun in her, now set,
her eyes that took him back, and in,
squinting as he squirmed, appraising,
    praising him again,

so that, when sifting through her basement
stacked with a dozen such false starts,
and lifting this one, lighter than
he thought it ought to be, to frame
    and hang in his apartment,

he saw in his flushed face how she'd
re-created there what rose
and fell in hers: the confidence
she forfeited each time she dared
    think of an audience.

Who (she must have asked) *would care?*
He does: that finished head conveys
still to him how, sought in a crowd,
a loved one stands apart—he's taller,
   comes in a different shade.

II

ELEGIES FOR ETSUKO

ELEGIES FOR ETSUKO

I

Begin with the last and unrecorded scene—
how rashly, with a length of rope,
she'd gathered up an end to hope?
Or unravel these six years
to where my life first tangled up with hers?
Or, midway, to that greater knot: again

the line of thought loops back, heart-
broken, to where she reckoned life to start.
Her wedding day. The Bride.
And in truth, that day I shed
a veil of happy tears: to see that snow
mountain of kimono

and, falling from the pinnacle
of her lacquered wig, the fog of silk
over a face too shy, too proud
to lift. Who'd made her up?—the natural
milk of her skin absorbed in chalk,
a slope of powder

down to her collar, pulled low at the back.
Viewed from behind, a woman's neck
is (say the Japanese—and so she'd say)
her most erotic feature.
But I think she was that day
a hybrid sort of fantasy, a creature

sparked by a wand, then shrinking like that star
when the TV goes black. Am I unkind?
Darling, we guess at how you came unwound;
at how many times you drunkenly replayed
that trade of sacred *sake* and were made
Queen for a Day again on the VCR.

II

Given how brief a spell
happiness usually is, and the ways
people are forever failing us,
with time it shocks me less you didn't mind
leaving the two of them behind;
yes yes, I see that, I see it very well . . .
But do you mean to say you were willing
never again to wear a new dress?
And never again to choose one for your daughter?
Long before she was born, or mine was,
we'd go on window-shopping sprees
in children's stores. Saccharine, but true.
I can't stand it, one of us would say; *can you?*
—A bonnet or a tasseled sock would send
us off: half-stifled, giggling cries . . .

In the end, you didn't think to find
even a rag to shield her eyes.
Because you had gone blind.

III

In Keiko's brain these words are Japanese
in bits and pieces   none of them is written
nobody's here to hear the words she knows
nobody's here   just Mother on the ceiling
her face is closed her face   long face her hair
not crying now   she tries *okaasan*   Mother
the word that calls up everything
and nothing moves at all   oh there's her ball

IV

Ages between the day I left Japan
and the first time I saw you again: the last
time, too. New Year's Eve in Rome.
Foreigners both, we soon pick up that wordless, winking giddiness we'd had: as light
a burden as our daughters, whom we lift
to watch the soaring fireworks. Each time the sky
blows up again, and then begins to cry
in sputters—whistling, molten streaks of tears—
we laugh: *See? Nothing to be afraid of* . . .
And in the window, too, we see ourselves
reflected kindly in our girls: *They'll learn*
to be mothers just like us. How long since you
were known as Hara-san (Miss Hara)! These days
it haunts me, that when you married you erased
your first name too—and as an honor asked

I call you by a childhood nickname, Ekko.
Ekko. Echo. *Ecco*: the champagne
cork pops, the skies explode, repeat
that automatic gunfire to the heart:
Ekko, who would not toast the year again.

V

These vacant months I've tried to disavow
that something's happened to you, something dire.
I know you're gone for good. And this is how

I've figured out you've made your final bow
(at last, the proof's so small that we require!)—
were you alive, you would have called by now.

More clues come than I'd willingly allow:
if they hadn't shoveled you into the fire
(I know you're gone for good, and this is how)

and buried you beneath a maple bough,
you would have dropped a line or sent a wire.
Were you alive, you would have called by now.

The phone's the lifeline of the lost *hausfrau*.
But now what's at your ear? The angel's lyre?
I know you're gone for good, and this is how

I turn the same line over like a plow,
since there is nothing further to inquire.
Were you alive, you would have called by now

to greet me in your faulty English grammar.
Your silence shows precisely how you are.
I know you're gone for good. And this is how:
were you alive, you would have called by now.

VI

Up here's where you end up. Room with a view
in (of all places) Edinburgh, though who's
willing to predict she'll feel at home
with dying anywhere? Why not the random
furnished flat in Scotland? What we own,
what we are owned by, are no less transient
than other plots of earth we briefly rent . . .

Parking across the street, we stay inside
as if we hope (we fear) you're still up there
in a state of mind precarious but alive:
you mustn't be allowed to think we're spying.
You seem to know I knew I'd have to come;
that your husband's brought me here, a half-year later.
Oh, anything we do may set the chain

reaction going once more in that brown
study of your brain; we'd have to live
through losing you again; we'd have to choose . . .
Why is it your apartment's set ablaze
and no one else's? Why is it in the pitch
of six o'clock in winter, nothing's on
in all the building—just the silhouette

of a woman coming slowly to your window
to watch the Christmas lights down Princes Street
illuminate toy people and their things?
. . . Unless, somehow, you're giving us the ghost
of a chance to guess how singularly bright
you'd felt yourself to burn, engulfed in flame
none of us ever saw, much less put out?

VII

Once, in Kyoto, we gossipped past the temple
graveyard where you'd lie, on to the shrine

where you wanted us to buy two paper dolls:
featureless, pure white, the kind a child

cuts in hand-holding chains across a fold.
An old priest had us sign them both for luck.

I wrote across the heart, you down the spine,
then quaintly (so I thought) you drew two smiles . . .

That was before you snapped your pretty neck.
Happy you may have been, but never simple.

VIII

Happy you may have been . . .
There were whole years when I'd have said
you were happier than anyone.
You've now been dead

(and been enclosed
in the double mystery of what
that is, and why you thought
it might be best)

for long enough it's time
to more than forgive the sin
of express despair, the crime
of not being what we seem,

or of not being anything
in particular . . . for isn't that
really what you feared you were?
Sometimes the note

you didn't write (because
you needed all the energy you had
to do the deed? because
there's no cause in the mad,

for whom the world's a small
footstool kicked aside?)
looms real and legible.
It says you died

because you'd come to think that love
is not enough. Well, I'd
probably have agreed,
advised you to find work, to read.

And now love's pain, your curse,
is all I have. Forgive me . . . What worse
punishment for suicide
than having died?

IX

On the master list we keep
imagining the scribes still keep
religiously, up there in space,
of every human life, let
them not neglect to fill the line
for Etsuko Akai, who's gone
    from Earth at twenty-eight.

In the impossible blue dark,
let all the bearded saints and rain-
bowed angels sorrow can invent
take her, who never made her mark,

and gladly mark the day for love
not of what she might have been,
    but what she humbly was.

For surely they have reams of time
to celebrate the perfect moon
set in her attentive face,
where pallidly, one shallow crater—
a pockmark time could not efface—
glossed the ancient and unwritten
    flaws of her Creator.

Since they will all be there for ages,
let them in their inventory
preserve in lucent, gilt-edged pages
those things I would myself record:
such as the way she'd tell a story—
she'd race, and trip, and laugh so hard
    we'd ask her to start over.

III

TIMEPIECES

THE MOON AND BIG BEN

STOP. Here, in our widened eyes,
they're nearly of a size.
And loom so close they seem to miss
    meeting by a nose,

the two moons of a pair of glasses
slowly disengaging as
the left one rises up to peer
    over the other's shoulder.

She finds there, in the Gothic news-
print of his measured face,
a daily mirror of the Times—
    the catalogue of crimes

and speeches, elections, electrocutions,
the columns and the revolutions
bringing new tyrannies to power
    almost by the hour—

and sees he stands for the imperial
notion of direction. The serial,
progressive sequence of events
    has, he booms, consequence.

Well. It is an ancient dial-
ectic, and it may take her awhile
(or forever) who whispers in his ear
    the limits of the linear

repeatedly, and every night,
to prove she has it right;
but there can be no gainsaying how,
  floating higher, smaller now

(and soon in ever-slimmer crescents),
she's not yet lost her essence.

A GRANDFATHER CLOCK

for Harold Leithauser

How long since he had wound it, or how often
he'd come down in the dark to pull the weight
of its three pendants, each a rising sun,
nobody knew. And now it was too late.
There it accused us, like an upright coffin,
of all the things we'd never thought to ask.
But soon his eldest son rose to his task,
opened the fragile panel like a surgeon,

tender in this invasion, and pulled down
the chains that snagged us—skipping like the sawn,
dry breath drawn after tears. The incomplete
cadence of a quarter hour—and then
his grandchildren, hearts busy as the snow
closing up the place where he had gone,
and flushed with all they knew and didn't know,
fleshed out the next hour playing at its feet.

DOUBLES

Months later, when she's begun to breathe
more easily without him, she exhumes
    a roll of film, like a mummy, from
the camera's black chamber. Her memory
    of everything, not only him,

    has gone a little fuzzy—that's
a price she's had to pay—and in a rush
    she drops it off at the shop like sheets
she hasn't time to launder. It's all the same
    in the chemical bath, the surfacing frame

    after frame of grandchild, sunrise, garden—
and all the same to the man who hands them back
    to her, thick and bland as a deck
of never-shuffled cards. Yet when she deals
    them out on that snowbound night, she finds—

    somewhat to her surprise—the days
(each fenced in commemorative white border)
    again at her fingertips, and in order:
leafing from winter into fall, and fall
    into summer, a movie run in reverse,

    she's happy. And then she slows like a hearse.
It's him. Oh God, it's him. She thought she'd given
    all of him away—his ties
to the boys, his hundred handkerchiefs, his shoes—
    but here he is. There's more of him to lose.

Receive it like his posthumous postcard—a "wish
I were here"? How long did this message, curled as if
in a bottle, wait to bring its proof
of some blue passage home from another world?
Who took this last, lost picture? She can't

remember. Rooted here in her boots,
she knows it can't have been herself: she's *there*,
in her tennis dress and fresh-permed hair;
she's living next to his seersucker shorts, the blinding
glint on his glasses, the shine on his balding head,

she's standing with him behind the net
and squinting into an unseen sun—or, now,
into the mirror of her own
face that has grown used to one alone.
Dear man. If she could kiss that hand—

the hand he's flung across her shoulder,
warm from the game . . . But she understands no feat
of athletic prowess will ever let
her jump that sagging net, and the game's unfair:
the two of them against the one of her.

PUZZLE PIECE

—Where was I? Somewhere in Michigan,
dozens of years ago, a Sunday . . .
The time all mixed in with the place,
as if neither might be found again
but in the other's hand. A day
for taking the children in the car,
time-consumingly and far,
somewhere designed to please.

"Look!" A sculptured garden. Pine
shaved to a cone; hedges a maze . . .
A lineup of tulips cheered our run
onto a field where lay a giant
floral clock whose face—radiant
from within as the brazen, fine-meshed wheel
of sun my brother drew at school—
called and called us in. It was

(or so it's seen now, peered at through
a peephole memory furnishes
in doors the long-grown vines rope shut)
that world upon a garnished platter
our parents wished to serve us.
Order gloved as Beauty, who
waved, waved from her parading float . . .
Was there already something the matter

that I'd remember this at all?
Shouldn't it have seemed natural
for the round of countless, fragrant hours
to be set by others into place,
an unpuzzled ground of flowers?
—Something having to do with his face
as my father, young, already going gray,
lifted me away?

A CHRISTMAS TREE

Dark. Still dark. But morning. Tip-
toeing down the steps, and half-asleep,
   I'm halfway there when it dawns

on me why I've come: the tree.
Had I left it on all night, like a green
   traffic signal that glows unread?

But each of its tiny lights is white.
I'd hung the three strands of them myself,
   like pearls looped head to foot,

and then, I remember, when we switched
them on, each pearl—as if wand-
   prompted—turned to diamond.

Behind, another image shines
in the window: stars complete with lines
   to constellate them wind the stair

of the tree that's barely mirrored there.
Too dark. I stretch out on the beach
   of a comfortable couch

and wait for the tree to pull me in.
But first, it flings out from its drawers
   every old, glad thing it has,

whether sacred or profane:
Santa, star, and candy cane,
   nutcracker, sleigh, and drum,

snowflake and rocking horse . . . It even
produces that ugly, papier-maché
   angel I made at seven.

He used to take great pride,
my father, crowning his tree with her crooked
   wire halo. Now we tend to hide

her somewhere near the back—and yet
I find I haven't thrown her out;
   a familiar, grown-up greed

not to have things but to feel intensely
happy and sad at once, as long
   as we get to keep on feeling,

radiates from me to the tree.
It gazes back as firm and steady
   as one who knows already

that, in a moment, when the balance tips
from gray to daylight, sending its hundred
   stars into eclipse,

I'll bury my head in this afghan, close
my eyes to reprint them there, and curl
   up to sleep like a girl.

I LOSE YOU FOR AN INSTANT

Guilin, China

The sun's at last soaking up
the rut-puddled street, and hundreds
of age-old, unoiled bicycles
together like thunder rip

over a hump of bridge.
Out of the blue, in another
military-mud-
green jeep conveying

what looks like body-bags
until one spills (just rice),
or heaps of gravel (why?
it's a mystery

nobody can unravel:
tons of it from nowhere,
and deposited in the most
God-forsaken spots—

in the midst of highways,
parking lots—as if in earnest
of an undone dynasty soon
to regroup from dust),

a horn's leaned on, less meant
to warn *Get out of my way*
than to exult *I'm driving . . .*
But the seas of bicycles part.

I'm standing on the bridge,
and under the black coat
packed that I might blend
into the bleakness I expected, am

five months pregnant.
I've dragged you all the way to China
(you dragging all our bags)
because I've been afraid

our days of exhilarating frights
are drawing to an end.
I'm scared, all right. I saw you run
into that crowd of rain-

ponchos, clouds of unlikely
pink and yellow,
after the blurred, blonde head
of a girl from our hotel—

calling to me behind
you'd find out where she'd found
her rented bicycle—
and now I think it's ten

minutes I've stood here,
round-eyed, round-bellied foreigner
whom nobody seems to mind.
It's just occurred to me

that I have both our passports, and
you have all our money.
You will come back. And time,
though it promises to fill

full the brave new world
with gravel, will deliver us
a daughter—as it braids another
river from a glossy fall

of rain; and chooses to preserve
as lovelier than then the often-
painted mountains of Guilin:
so steep they ought

to come to pencil-points.
High parentheses
(enclosing that lost
instant), they rise mis-

shapen in my eyes.

SUMMER 1983

None of us remembers these, the days
when passing strangers adored us at first sight,
just for living, or for strolling down the street;
praised all our given names; begged us to smile . . .
you, too, in a little while,
my darling, will have lost all this,
asked for a kiss will give one, and learn
how love dooms us to earn
love once we can speak of it.

EMILY WANTS TO PLAY

That alarming cry—
and before I even understand
I'm up, I've stumbled down the hall
   to where she lies in wait on her back,
   smiling. She's fooled me again.
     By the digital clock
it's 2:53 in the morning, and
   Emily wants to play.

   She rustles in
sheer happiness, under quilts I peel
back to take her up, up,
   and into the crook of my arm,
   where she's far too thrilled to settle.
     She wants no bottle,
shrugs off my gentle rocking—no,
   she'd rather squirm

    to face those two
red eyes dividing hour from minute,
staring at hers as if they know
   how blue they'll grow by day.
   As she turns to me
     I look away,
with a heavy nod to illustrate
   We're sleeping now, see?

But see she does,
her eyes a magnifying glass
to burn my eyes in shame: she's had
   time already to learn
that nighttime is for love.
   Wakefulness
touches me gladly now, the thought
   of the giant yellow moon

   the night she was born,
and later, come winter, how
I nursed her by the light of snow
   ticking against this window.
   Having won me at last,
      she yawns; she's been vigilant
as this memory of her that can't
   rest until set down.

AUBADE FOR BRAD

At six o'clock begins the ritual dance
of bumping into bureaus in the dark;
     it's time you went to work.
Holding one shoe at arm's length like a candle,
you grope for its mate, but stumbling on a sandal
     of mine, abandon hope
and ask for guidance in the softest voice;
I whisper too, as if there's still a chance
     we might not wake me up.

Once shod, you pull the creaking blinds whose slats
narrow their sleepy eyelids into slits,
     and I'm to take the cue
more sloth is my reward for finding you
the means by which you'll disappear till dinner.
     Condemned to write
from dawn until you drop in bed at night,
you'll spend a happy, virtuous day convinced
     you are a miserable sinner.

No doubt it is the hard fate of the Writer
to suffer like the rest, but not know better
     than to call it a job. What's worse
than feeling so deeply one must doubly force
oneself to show it in both prose and verse?
     I sympathize, of course;
so much, in fact, I'd joyfully disprove
that formula by which all Energy
     converts to (Printed) Matter

and devote, this morning, some of it to Love.
    Darling, if you'll untie
    your shoes again and lie
for a moment here, while the sun turns all to gold,
    I may grow very bold.

CHERNOBYL

Once upon a time,
the word alone was scary.
Now, quainter than this rhyme,
it's the headline of a story

long yellowed in the news.
The streets were hosed in Kiev,
and Poles took more shampoos.
The evacuees were brave.

Under the gay striped awning
of Europe's common market,
half-empty booths were yawning
at the small change in the pocket.

As far away as Rome,
unseen through weeks of sun,
the cloud kept children home.
Milk gurgled down the drain.

In Wales, spring lambs were painted
blue, not to be eaten
till next spring when . . . Still tainted,
they'd grown into blue mutton.

Then we had had enough.
Fear's harder to retain
than hope or indifference. Safe
and innocent, the rain

fell all night as we slept,
and the story at last was dead—
all traces of it swept
under the earth's green bed.

ARMISTICE DAY

Have I shown you these before?
                    Well, here's another
album of the wounded soldiers Mother
was sketching then, the last year of the war.
That would be World War Two—before the days
of photocopies. All these are snapshots of
the originals in charcoal, which she'd give
to the men themselves, of course. And I suppose
we're better off to have the photos, if
the way this paper they've been pasted on
has yellowed now is any indication.
What always strikes me, though, is how much life
she seemed to draw from them, these sorry boys
turbanned in bandages (or in the case
of many—though we're only shown the face—
legless or armless, I would guess).
And many knew they wouldn't last forever—
you can be sure of that. But for a while
they gave her, one by one, the unfeigned smile
a young man (with the bravery of fever
burning in his face) will give a woman
who's come, by magic, to sit beside his bed.

Your grandmother—you've seen her pictures—had
that effect on people. Not just on the men.
But that's not what I brought these out to say . . .
The other night, when I discovered these
(or rediscovered; why it should surprise
me, year by year, to find how they
are still just where I left them, with the other

memorabilia crammed there on that shelf,
is a mystery I'm sure I'll never solve!),
I wasn't thinking mostly of my mother,
but of the look of *them*: the packs of boys
lined up like cards, four down and four across,
pages and pages of the Flying Aces,
the G.I. Jacks, and more of them whose faces—
whose days—were numbered . . . Maybe I was asleep
when all these images began to come
tauntingly to me, as if a game
of sickeningly clever luck were up
to me to stop. In any case, I failed,
and sleep (if that is what it was, that night,
making my vision swim) transformed the white
pages to cream, to mustard-colored field

after field of headstones.
                            Unmarked. Horrible
(I wonder if you feel it!) to have their heads
and not their names. Names can be repeated . . .
But as if each head were answering to the roll
call of the Unknown Soldier, I saw—as in
this one, for instance, looking down his nose
comically, you have to think, or this
handsomer one, with the distinguished chin—
how well-known each of us is to himself.
How famous all our mothers . . . Well, Emily,
I suppose that when you're older you may feel
it was foolish of me, keeping albums full
of strangers, as if I thought of them as family.
You may decide you have no room. Imagine:

the day they signed the Armistice (September
second, 1945: remember
that one, won't you?) Mother was twenty-one.
Her birthday. And although she lost her chance
on a trip to Europe (the USO had planned
to send her, before the war came to an end),
what a party they all had! She loved to dance,
and she told me how they danced all through that night . . .
Strangers kissed each other in the street.

IV

DEAD LETTERS

DEAD LETTERS

I

Dear Mrs. Salter: Congratulations! You
(no need to read on—yet I always do)
may have won the sweepstakes, if you'll send . . .
Is this how it must end?
Or will it ever end? The bills, all paid,
come monthly anyway, to cheer the dead.
BALANCE: decimal point and double o's
like pennies no one placed upon your eyes.
I never saw you dead—you simply vanished,
your body gone to Science, as you wished:
I was the one to send you there, by phone,
on that stunned morning answering the blunt
young nurse who called, wanting to "clear the room."
"Take her," I said, "I won't be coming in"—
couldn't bear to see your cherished face with more
death in it than was there five days before.
But now, where are you really? From the mail
today, it seems, you might almost be well:
Dear Patient: It's been three years since your eyes
were checked . . . A host of worthy causes vies
for your attention: endangered wildlife funds,
orphans with empty bowls in outstretched hands,
political prisoners, Congressmen. The *LAST*
*ISSUE*s of magazines are never last.
And now you've shored up on some realtors' list,
since word went out you've "moved" to my address:
Dear New Apartment Owner: If you rent . . .
Mother, in daydreams sometimes I am sent

to follow you, my own forwarding text
Dear Mrs. Salter's Daughter: You are next.

II

When I try to concentrate
on who you were,
images of you blur
and pulsate, like the clothes
left in your closet—

every size from four to fourteen,
not progressively,
but back and forth again:
testaments to Treatment
after Treatment.

Injected, radiated,
bloated, balded, nauseated;
years in an iron wig that ill
fit or befitted you;
then more years, unexpected,

of a cobweb gray you grew
in thanks to covet:
lurching from reprieve to reprieve,
you taught yourself to live
with less and less,

and so did we—
even, at last, without the giddy
vastness of your love,
so painfully withdrawn when pain
became all you could think of.

Trying not to feel
that nothing, not even love
or death, is original,
like other mourners I've
turned up happy photographs—

of the ruby-lipsticked girl
(in black-and-white, but I can tell)
on your wedding day; or, here, a scene
in a hallway I'd hardly know was ours
but for that gilt barometer.

Had I lost that about you?
Your regal touch—china in green
and gold; silk Oriental dresses?
. . . Days that made you queen
of nothing but your high-backed bed

convinced you
you'd been singled out to die.
Yet here you are,
a smiling hostess at the door
bidding your friends goodbye:

What blessedness!
—To think that once
you hadn't had to be the focus,
could go on living unpitied,
even unnoticed.

III

Dinner in Boston. I am twenty-three,
and you have come to see
your grown-up daughter in her element.
My choice is cheap and almost elegant:
crêpes and spinach salad, a carafe
of chilled house wine we laugh

companionably over. Memory drifts
back to well-set tables shared at home—
those animated dinners you would chair
(the Salter Seminars, my boyfriend called them)
where you taught me to admire
the complex givens of your gifts

for life. Accomplished cook,
stickler for decorum, you liked to shock
us with the heedless, vocal sweep
of your opinions: on the Catholic Church
(you hate it, so you think—hate it so much
you'll find a slow way back);

the saintliness of Adlai; Armageddon.
(Once, you greeted me from school with news
the Chinese had invaded us: a thrill
that never found its way to print,
but you shrugged off my complaint:
"If they haven't done it yet, you know they will.")

Tonight, Newbury Street—
scene of my happy lunch hours, of the young
executives with ice cream cones
dripping down their hands, bright students in new jeans—
outside our window takes, as night sifts down,
that memorializing cast of light

you seem to shed on things, all by yourself.
Even when all is well (the illness
more under control than less,
you're devoting all your time to sculpture
bigger than you are—filling every shelf
in the garage!) I still recapture

moments before they're over.
She loved me so, that when I praised her shirt
she took it off her back, or
We drank four cups of tea apiece . . . Alert
always to what perishes, I invert
your low, confiding chuckle now and pour

its darkness like a stain across our table.
"Can you remember Grandma's laugh? I can't,"
I interrupt, and having voiced the fear,
immediately am able:
it sounded like a baby's xylophone,
thrown down a flight of stairs.

Who could have forgotten *that?*
I laugh myself—but now I've spoiled
the mood, or turned it oversweet,
and you reach into your magic purse
for a snapshot of your mother. "Here, it's yours."
Stunned how soon my eyes have filled

with tears—how easy it has been
to give a pleasing answer—
you seem relieved to put to death
a momentary fright not only mine.
Now, your own forever-
unrecorded voice cut short by cancer,

I still find myself asking: dear
as she was, didn't you know
it's you I was crying for?

IV

We're on our way to the hospital
for the twenty-thousandth time.
You used to drive—then I;
lately, we've piled into a taxi.
Each week a new man takes the rap
for bumps and jolts; if not for him
(you imply) we'd have a pleasant trip.
Shrunken and old, collapsible,
head in my lap, you start up in alarm:
"Mary Jo—I think I'm ill."

Forgive me that I laughed!
It's too late to apologize;
but that you could find it in you still
to register surprise—
that *you'd* hope to be well . . .
It kept you alive, of course,
those years of asking visitors
"Are your ears ringing?" as if there might
someday be found a blanket cause
for pains that kept you up all night.

V

If you could see your daughter, no green thumb,
tending the philodendron
you sent me when my baby girl was born!
If you could see my daughter: that refrain
twists like a crimping weed, a vine of pain
around the joy of everything she learns.

And yet it intertwines
forever, I perceive, your life and mine.
From time to time, a heart-shaped leaf will turn
yellow and fall—in falling a leaf torn
out of your life again,
the story I must constantly revive.

I water it and live;
water and wait for other plants to bloom.
I took them from your room
nearly a year ago now, poinsettias
of that wizened, stricken Christmas
you floated through five days before the end.

One's inky-red; the other paper-white . . .
You too were one to note
life's artful correspondences.
But I can't let them go,
not yet; and granted time to tend
a growing tenderness, I send

more letters, Mother—these despite
the answers you can't write.

A NOTE ABOUT THE AUTHOR

Mary Jo Salter was born in Grand Rapids, Michigan, was raised in Detroit and Baltimore, and was educated at Harvard and Cambridge University. Her first book of poems, *Henry Purcell in Japan*, was published by Alfred A. Knopf in 1985.

She has been the recipient of a National Endowment for the Arts Fellowship, was a co-winner of the Discovery/The Nation prize, and was a poet-in-residence at the Frost Place. Her poems have appeared in *The New Yorker*, *The Atlantic*, *Grand Street*, *The New Republic*, and *Yale Review*, among others.

In the past decade she has spent extensive periods abroad —in Kyoto, Rome, and London. She lives now in Reykjavik, Iceland, with her husband, the writer Brad Leithauser, and their two daughters, Emily and Hilary.

A NOTE ON THE TYPE

The text of this book was set on the Linotype in Fairfield, a typeface designed by the distinguished artist and engraver, Rudolph Ruzicka (1883–1978). Fairfield is the creation of a master craftsman whose type designs exhibit a singular clarity and simplicity which have earned them a permanent place in the typographic repertory.

Ruzicka was born in Bohemia and came to America in 1894. He designed and illustrated many books (including a number for Alfred A. Knopf) and was the creator of a considerable list of individual prints in a variety of techniques.

Composed by Heritage Printers, Inc., Charlotte, North Carolina. Printed and bound by Halliday Lithographers, West Hanover, Massachusetts.